THE SONGS OF ANDREW LLOYD WEBBER™

40 OF HIS GREATES

Note: the keys in this book do not match the other wind instruments

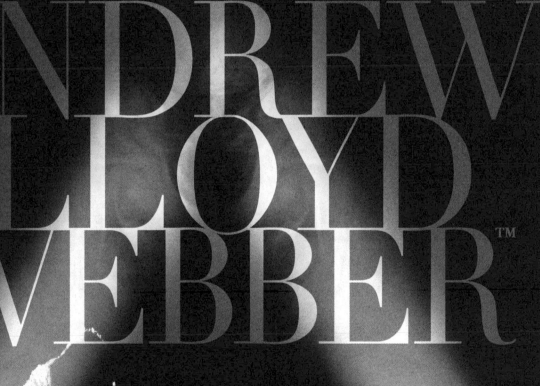

ANDREW LLOYD WEBBER™

Andrew Lloyd Webber™ is a trademark owned by Andrew Lloyd Webber.

ISBN 978-1-4768-1401-8

HAL•LEONARD®
7777 W. BLUEMOUND RD. P.O. BOX 13819 MILWAUKEE, WI 53213

In Australia Contact:
Hal Leonard Australia Pty. Ltd.
4 Lentara Court
Cheltenham, Victoria, 3192 Australia
Email: ausadmin@halleonard.com.au

Visit Hal Leonard Online at
www.halleonard.com

CONTENTS

ALL I ASK OF YOU

from THE PHANTOM OF THE OPERA

TENOR SAX

Music by ANDREW LLOYD WEBBER
Lyrics by CHARLES HART
Additional Lyrics by RICHARD STILGOE

ANOTHER SUITCASE IN ANOTHER HALL
from EVITA

TENOR SAX

Words by TIM RICE
Music by ANDREW LLOYD WEBBER

AMIGOS PARA SIEMPRE
(Friends for Life)
(The Official Theme of the Barcelona 1992 Games)

TENOR SAX

Music by ANDREW LLOYD WEBBER
Lyrics by DON BLACK

(small notes optional)

ANGEL OF MUSIC

from THE PHANTOM OF THE OPERA

TENOR SAX

Music by ANDREW LLOYD WEBBER
Lyrics by CHARLES HART
Additional Lyrics by RICHARD STILGOE

ANY DREAM WILL DO

from JOSEPH AND THE AMAZING TECHNICOLOR® DREAMCOAT

TENOR SAX

Music by ANDREW LLOYD WEBBER
Lyrics by TIM RICE

AS IF WE NEVER SAID GOODBYE
from SUNSET BOULEVARD

TENOR SAX

Music by ANDREW LLOYD WEBBER
Lyrics by DON BLACK and CHRISTOPHER HAMPTON,
with contributions by AMY POWERS

CLOSE EVERY DOOR

from JOSEPH AND THE AMAZING TECHNICOLOR® DREAMCOAT

TENOR SAX

Music by ANDREW LLOYD WEBBER
Lyrics by TIM RICE

Moderately, expressively

DON'T CRY FOR ME ARGENTINA

from EVITA

TENOR SAX

Words by TIM RICE
Music by ANDREW LLOYD WEBBER

EVERYTHING'S ALRIGHT

from *JESUS CHRIST SUPERSTAR*

TENOR SAX

Words by TIM RICE
Music by ANDREW LLOYD WEBBER

I DON'T KNOW HOW TO LOVE HIM
from JESUS CHRIST SUPERSTAR

TENOR SAX

Words by TIM RICE
Music by ANDREW LLOYD WEBBER

HIGH FLYING, ADORED

from EVITA

TENOR SAX

Words by TIM RICE
Music by ANDREW LLOYD WEBBER

I AM THE STARLIGHT

from STARLIGHT EXPRESS

TENOR SAX

Music by ANDREW LLOYD WEBBER
Lyrics by RICHARD STILGOE

I BELIEVE MY HEART
from THE WOMAN IN WHITE

TENOR SAX

Music by ANDREW LLOYD WEBBER
Lyrics by DAVID ZIPPEL

I'M HOPELESS WHEN IT COMES TO YOU

from STEPHEN WARD

TENOR SAX

Music by ANDREW LLOYD WEBBER
Book and Lyrics by DON BLACK
and CHRISTOPHER HAMPTON

Freely

LEARN TO BE LONELY
from THE PHANTOM OF THE OPERA

TENOR SAX

Music by ANDREW LLOYD WEBBER
Lyrics by CHARLES HART

LIGHT AT THE END OF THE TUNNEL

from STARLIGHT EXPRESS

TENOR SAX

Music by ANDREW LLOYD WEBBER
Lyrics by RICHARD STILGOE

LOVE CHANGES EVERYTHING

from ASPECTS OF LOVE

TENOR SAX

Music by ANDREW LLOYD WEBBER
Lyrics by DON BLACK and CHARLES HART

(small notes optional)

MEMORY
from CATS

TENOR SAX

Music by ANDREW LLOYD WEBBER
Text by TREVOR NUNN after T.S. ELIOT

LOVE NEVER DIES

from LOVE NEVER DIES

TENOR SAX

Music by ANDREW LLOYD WEBBER
Lyrics by GLENN SLATER

MAKE UP MY HEART
from STARLIGHT EXPRESS

TENOR SAX

Music by ANDREW LLOYD WEBBER
Lyrics by RICHARD STILGOE

MR. MISTOFFELEES
from CATS

TENOR SAX

Music by ANDREW LLOYD WEBBER
Text by T.S. ELIOT

THE MUSIC OF THE NIGHT
from THE PHANTOM OF THE OPERA

TENOR SAX

Music by ANDREW LLOYD WEBBER
Lyrics by CHARLES HART
Additional Lyrics by RICHARD STILGOE

NO MATTER WHAT
from WHISTLE DOWN THE WIND

TENOR SAX

Music by ANDREW LLOYD WEBBER
Lyrics by JIM STEINMAN

THE PERFECT YEAR
from SUNSET BOULEVARD

TENOR SAX

Music by ANDREW LLOYD WEBBER
Lyrics by DON BLACK
and CHRISTOPHER HAMPTON

THE PHANTOM OF THE OPERA
from THE PHANTOM OF THE OPERA

TENOR SAX

Music by ANDREW LLOYD WEBBER
Lyrics by CHARLES HART
Additional Lyrics by RICHARD STILGOE
and MIKE BATT

Moderately fast

PIE JESU
from REQUIEM

TENOR SAX

By ANDREW LLOYD WEBBER

STARLIGHT EXPRESS
from STARLIGHT EXPRESS

TENOR SAX

Music by ANDREW LLOYD WEBBER
Lyrics by RICHARD STILGOE

Moderately

THE POINT OF NO RETURN

from THE PHANTOM OF THE OPERA

TENOR SAX

Music by ANDREW LLOYD WEBBER
Lyrics by CHARLES HART
Additional Lyrics by RICHARD STILGOE

(small notes optional)

SEEING IS BELIEVING

from ASPECTS OF LOVE

TENOR SAX

Music by ANDREW LLOYD WEBBER
Lyrics by DON BLACK and CHARLES HART

(small notes optional)

STICK IT TO THE MAN

from SCHOOL OF ROCK

TENOR SAX

Music by ANDREW LLOYD WEBBER
Lyrics by GLENN SLATER

(small notes optional)

SUPERSTAR

from *JESUS CHRIST SUPERSTAR*

TENOR SAX

Words by TIM RICE
Music by ANDREW LLOYD WEBBER

Lively Rock

TELL ME ON A SUNDAY

from SONG & DANCE

TENOR SAX

Music by ANDREW LLOYD WEBBER
Lyrics by DON BLACK

TAKE THAT LOOK OFF YOUR FACE
from SONG & DANCE

TENOR SAX

Music by ANDREW LLOYD WEBBER
Lyrics by DON BLACK

49

THINK OF ME
from THE PHANTOM OF THE OPERA

TENOR SAX

Music by ANDREW LLOYD WEBBER
Lyrics by CHARLES HART
Additional Lyrics by RICHARD STILGOE

'TIL I HEAR YOU SING

from LOVE NEVER DIES

TENOR SAX

Music by ANDREW LLOYD WEBBER
Lyrics by GLENN SLATER

Moderately

(small notes optional)

UNEXPECTED SONG
from SONG & DANCE

TENOR SAX

Music by ANDREW LLOYD WEBBER
Lyrics by DON BLACK

(small notes optional)

WHISTLE DOWN THE WIND

from WHISTLE DOWN THE WIND

TENOR SAX

Music by ANDREW LLOYD WEBBER
Lyrics by JIM STEINMAN

WISHING YOU WERE SOMEHOW HERE AGAIN

from THE PHANTOM OF THE OPERA

TENOR SAX

Music by ANDREW LLOYD WEBBER
Lyrics by CHARLES HART
Additional Lyrics by RICHARD STILGOE

(small notes optional)

WITH ONE LOOK

from SUNSET BOULEVARD

TENOR SAX

Music by ANDREW LLOYD WEBBER
Lyrics by DON BLACK and CHRISTOPHER HAMPTON,
with contributions by AMY POWERS

YOU MUST LOVE ME

from the Cinergi Motion Picture EVITA

Words by TIM RICE
Music by ANDREW LLOYD WEBBER

TENOR SAX

Moderately